The First Day of
Winter

by Gordon L. Storey
illustrated by Kathy Couri

Scott Foresman

Editorial Offices: Glenview, Illinois • New York, New York
Sales Offices: Reading, Massachusetts • Duluth, Georgia
Glenview, Illinois • Carrollton, Texas • Menlo Park, California

"It is winter!" said Bunny.
"I like winter so much!
Let's go out."

"It is winter," said Mama.

"So you need to dress warm.

Then we can go out."

"Do you have any shirts?
Here they are," said Mama.
"Put on about four of them.
Put this one over that one."

"I can do that," said Bunny.
And he did.

"Do you have any warm pants?
Here they are," said Mama.
"Put on about three of them.
Put this one over that one."

"I can do that," said Bunny.

And he did.

"Do you have any sweaters?
Here they are," said Mama.
"Put on about three of them.
Put this one over that one."

"I can do that," said Bunny.
And he did.

"Do you have any thick socks?
Here they are," said Mama.
"Put on about six of them.
Put this one over that one."

"I can do that," said Bunny.
And he did.

"Do you have any fat mittens?
Here they are," said Mama.
"Put on about four of them.
Put this one over that one."

"I can do that," said Bunny.
And he did.

"Do you have a hat and a scarf?
Do you have your boots?
Here they are," said Mama.
"Let me help you."

"There!" said Mama.

"Now let's go out."

"I can't do that," said Bunny.

"Why not?" Mama asked.

"I can't get up!"